The Llandudno [illegible] Bay
Electric Railw[illegible]

[illegible]
Brian Hurst

NORTHERN PUBLISHING SERVICES

Published by Northern Publishing Services

ISBN 1 899181 09 1

Postcards from the collection of Bryan Hurst

Edited by

Cliff Hayes

Cover photograph: *A toast-rack picks up in Colwyn Bay, c.1950.*

Printed and bound by: Manchester Free Press.
Longford Trading Estate,
Thomas Street, Stretford,
Manchester M32 0JT.
Tel: 061-864 4540

INTRODUCTION

The cards are arranged as a journey from end to end of the tramway (Electric Railway). Starting at the Old Colwyn terminus, the images take us slowly down the line to Llandudno's West Shore. They move around in time but faithfully follow the route.

So come on board, settle down to a pleasant journey, not only for the enthusiasts and local people, but to view an era when life was slower and certainly more elegant.

DEDICATION

To my wife Rosemary who has patiently accompanied me on my travels all over the country in my quest for postcards.

THE LLANDUDNO AND COLWYN BAY ELECTRIC RAILWAY 1907-1956

After numerous failed attempts beginning in 1894, construction of the line between the two towns finally started in 1906; and the first tram entered Llandudno on 19th October 1907. It was not until 7th June 1908 that the service came to fruition from the Depot at Church Road, Llandudno, to the terminus at Station Road in Colwyn Bay. On 26th march 1915 the line was opened up to the Queen's Hotel in Old Colwyn, but due to the narrow roads through Old Colwyn and competition from motor buses, the line from Greenfield Road to the Queen's Hotel was closed on 21st September 1930.

During the Second World War the tramway witnessed a great increase in business. This was due to Civil Service branches moving to the area, American armed forces which were based in the area, and finally because of the withdrawal of buses from services. The end of the War saw the start of the decline in fortunes of the Company; increased competition from buses, sea damage to the track in Penryn Bay and the ruling by the Department of Transport forbidding the Company's two 'Darwin' trams from carrying passengers over Penrhyn Hill, were all factors which combined to see the end of the trams. And the end came on Saturday 24th March, 1956 when the last tram left Colwyn Bay for the depot, a sad day, not only for the locals but for the holiday makers too.

This book brings together the best of the old pictures and postcards of this unique piece of history that might have rivalled the famous Blackpool trams.

POST CARD

FOR CORRESPONDENCE

FOR ADDRESS ONLY

NORTHERN PUBLISHING SERVICES

The Llandudno and Colwyn Bay Electric Railway – 1907-1956

OLD COLWYN TERMINUS (c.1916)

Double trolley tram turning at the terminus outside the Queen's Hotel, Old Colwyn. This section of the line closed in 1930.

ABERGELE ROAD, OLD COLWYN.

POST CARD

FOR CORRESPONDENCE

FOR ADDRESS ONLY

NORTHERN PUBLISHING SERVICES

The Llandudno and Colwyn Bay Electric Railway – 1907-1956

ABERGELE ROAD, OLD COLWYN (c.1920)
Looking eastwards down Abergele Road.
The narrowness of track speeded this sections closure in 1930.

POST CARD

FOR CORRESPONDENCE

FOR ADDRESS ONLY

NORTHERN PUBLISHING SERVICES

The Llandudno and Colwyn Bay Electric Railway – 1907-1956

COLWYN BAY (c.1935)
One of the Company's Bournemouth double deckers about to begin its journey. The tracks to old Colwyn have now vanished.

LLANDUDNO
LLANDUDNO PIER
TRAM
STOP

POST CARD

FOR CORRESPONDENCE

FOR ADDRESS ONLY

NORTHERN PUBLISHING SERVICES

The Llandudno and Colwyn Bay Electric Railway – 1907-1956

COLWYN BAY (c.1950)

One of four 'Toast Racks' used in the summer. No.19 oustide St. Paul's Church, before starting its thirty-minute journey.

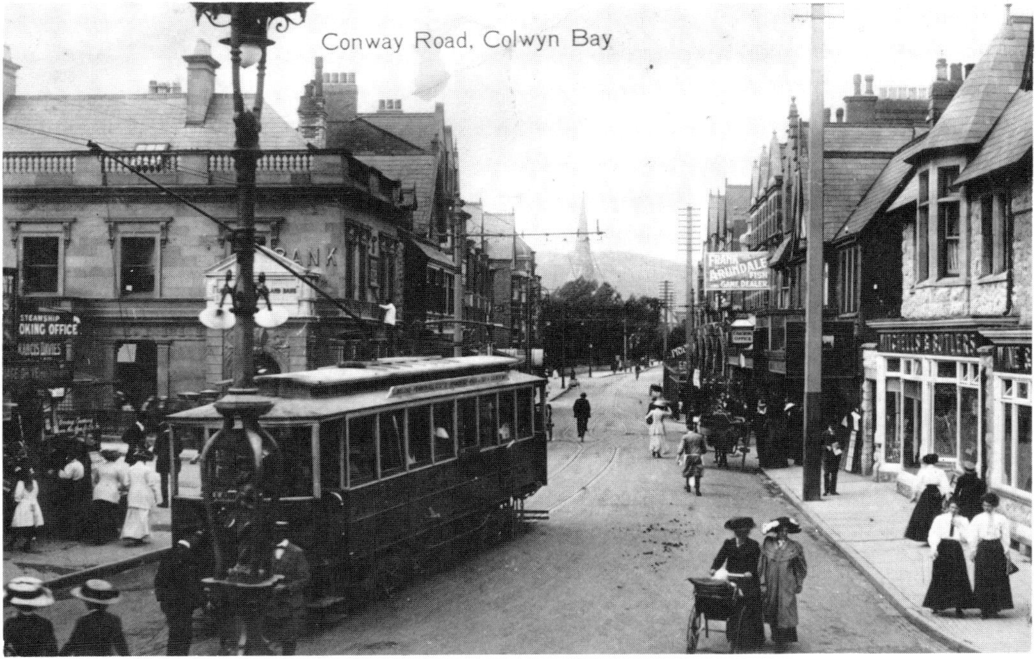

Conway Road, Colwyn Bay

POST CARD

FOR CORRESPONDENCE

FOR ADDRESS ONLY

NORTHERN PUBLISHING SERVICES
The Llandudno and Colwyn Bay Electric Railway – 1907-1956

CONWAY ROAD, COLWYN BAY (1913)
This was the terminus at the top of Station Road. Note the absence of motor transport, and the Steamship Booking Office on the left.

COACHING OFFICE
DAIRY
Book Here
BOOK HERE
Tram Terminus. Colwyn Bay.

POST CARD

FOR CORRESPONDENCE

FOR ADDRESS ONLY

NORTHERN PUBLISHING SERVICES

The Llandudno and Colwyn Bay Electric Railway – 1907-1956

COLWYN BAY TRAM TERMINUS (c.1908)
A view of the Station Road terminus looking towards Rhos-on-Sea. The Coach Booking Offices in opposition across the road.

POST CARD

FOR CORRESPONDENCE

FOR ADDRESS ONLY

NORTHERN PUBLISHING SERVICES

The Llandudno and Colwyn Bay Electric Railway – 1907-1956

CONWAY ROAD, COLWYN BAY (c.1955)
Single decker No.2 makes its way past Conway Road School and down the steady incline into the West End.

POST CARD

FOR CORRESPONDENCE

FOR ADDRESS ONLY

NORTHERN PUBLISHING SERVICES

The Llandudno and Colwyn Bay Electric Railway – 1907-1956

BRYN-EURYN (1910)

One of the original double trolley trams proceeds past Llanrch Road West, down Brompton Avenue towards Rhos-on Sea. Note the wide open spaces!

Whitehall Road, Rhos, Colwyn Bay
STOP

POST CARD

FOR CORRESPONDENCE

FOR ADDRESS ONLY

NORTHERN PUBLISHING SERVICES

The Llandudno and Colwyn Bay Electric Railway – 1907-1956

WHITEHALL ROAD, RHOS (c.1920)

Car No.1 approaches the Promenade. In the background is the Mount Stewart Hotel and on the right is Aberhod.

Promenade, Rhos-on-Sea, Colwyn Bay
ERS.
NEILL
CHEMIST
CHEMIST

POST CARD

FOR CORRESPONDENCE

FOR ADDRESS ONLY

NORTHERN PUBLISHING SERVICES
The Llandudno and Colwyn Bay Electric Railway – 1907-1956

PROMENADE, RHOS-ON-SEA (c.1920)
Car No.1 leaving the Promenade. Notice Rhos Pier in the background. Purchased from the Isle of Man only to be dismantled in the mid 1950s.

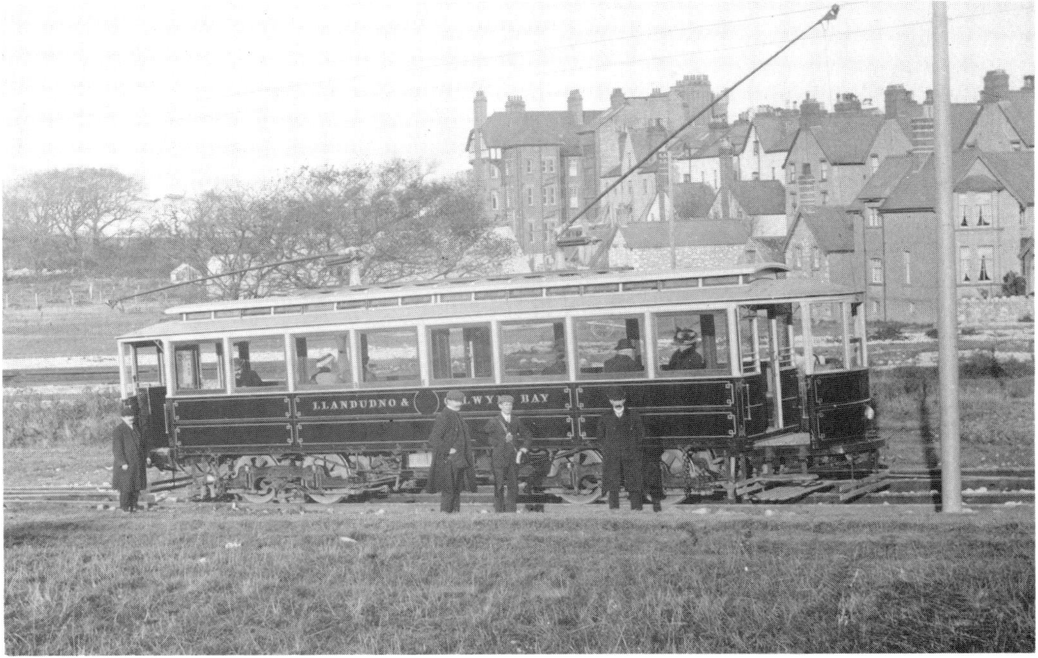
LLANDUDNO &
BAY

POST CARD

FOR CORRESPONDENCE

FOR ADDRESS ONLY

NORTHERN PUBLISHING SERVICES
The Llandudno and Colwyn Bay Electric Railway – 1907-1956

RHOS-ON-SEA (c.1907)
A very early postcard, an original car stopped on Penrhyn Avenue. The large building in the background is the Rhos Abbey Hotel.

ALMOND CRISPS
ALMOND CRISPS

POST CARD

FOR CORRESPONDENCE

FOR ADDRESS ONLY

NORTHERN PUBLISHING SERVICES

The Llandudno and Colwyn Bay Electric Railway – 1907-1956

THE DEPOT, RHOS ON SEA (early 1950s)
Car No.9 awaits outside the Depot at Church Road for a change of crew. The Depot is now a Road Haulage centre.

POST CARD

FOR CORRESPONDENCE

FOR ADDRESS ONLY

NORTHERN PUBLISHING SERVICES

The Llandudno and Colwyn Bay Electric Railway – 1907-1956

STAFF PHOTOGRAPH (c.1920)

Uniform was important and reflected status (note the army badges) as they pose proudly for this picture – complete with dog.

TOLL ROAD
COACHES & BUSES
2/6
THIS
LIGHT RAILWAY
RUNS ON
PRIVATE TRACK
IT IS NOT
A PUBLIC
HIGHWAY
L.& C.B.E.Rly LTD
DANGER
PLEASE DRIVE CAREFULLY
OPEN GATES
TRAM
STOP

POST CARD

FOR CORRESPONDENCE

FOR ADDRESS ONLY

NORTHERN PUBLISHING SERVICES

The Llandudno and Colwyn Bay Electric Railway – 1907-1956

RHOS-ON-SEA (c. 1950s)

The stretch of road to the west of Penhryn Avenue was owned by the Tram Company. The sign warns oncoming traffic of the tolls.

POST CARD

FOR CORRESPONDENCE

FOR ADDRESS ONLY

NORTHERN PUBLISHING SERVICES
The Llandudno and Colwyn Bay Electric Railway – 1907-1956

RHOS GOLF LINKS (c.1909)

Passing the Golf Course. This stretch was often covered by shingle brought up by rough seas. Services were interrupted until the line was cleared.

GLAN-Y-MOR ROAD, PENRHYN BAY.
22374?

POST CARD

FOR CORRESPONDENCE

FOR ADDRESS ONLY

NORTHERN PUBLISHING SERVICES
The Llandudno and Colwyn Bay Electric Railway – 1907-1956

GLAN-Y-MOR ROAD, PENRHYN BAY
A double trolley car makes its way past the Manager's (Mr Hamilton) house on the left, so all personnel had to be on their best behaviour when passing this area.

← Old Road
GARAGE
PENRHYN HILL.
2237

POST CARD

FOR CORRESPONDENCE

FOR ADDRESS ONLY

NORTHERN PUBLISHING SERVICES

The Llandudno and Colwyn Bay Electric Railway – 1907-1956

PENRHYN HILL, PENRHYN BAY (1940s)

The bottom of Penrhyn Hill and the tram climbing what is the east-bound side of the dual carriageway.

Tram Car passing Penrhynsioe. Llandudno.
LLANDUDNO & COLWYN BAY

POST CARD

FOR CORRESPONDENCE

FOR ADDRESS ONLY

NORTHERN PUBLISHING SERVICES

The Llandudno and Colwyn Bay Electric Railway – 1907-1956

PENRHYN HILL (c.1915)

Car No.4 posed against a background of the village of Penrhynside, whilst below Penrhyn Old Hall is clearly visible.

POST CARD

FOR CORRESPONDENCE

FOR ADDRESS ONLY

NORTHERN PUBLISHING SERVICES
The Llandudno and Colwyn Bay Electric Railway – 1907-1956

PENRHYN HILL FROM PENRHNYSIDE (1940s)
View from the top of Penhryn Hill. Llandrill-yn-Rhos in the background shows signs of becoming populated.

VIEW OF GREAT ORME AND BAY FROM

POST CARD

FOR CORRESPONDENCE

FOR ADDRESS ONLY

NORTHERN PUBLISHING SERVICES

The Llandudno and Colwyn Bay Electric Railway – 1907-1956

THE LOOP, PENRHYN HILL (c.1920)
Car No.11 stationary on the western side of Penrhyn Hill, waiting for the car from Colwyn Bay to arrive at the 'loop' where they pass one another.

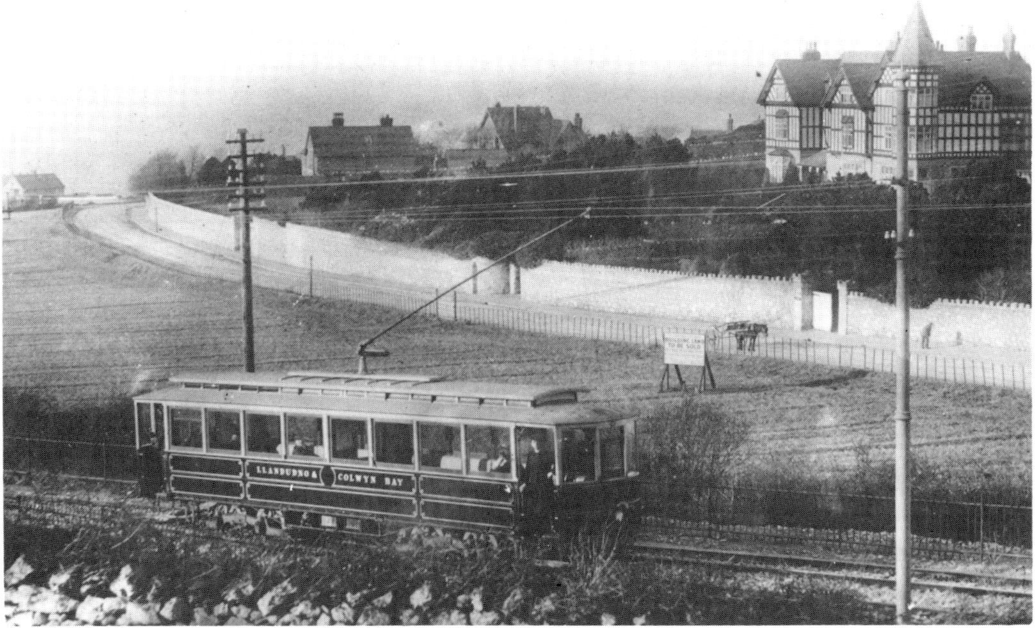
LLANDUDNO & COLWYN BAY

POST CARD

FOR CORRESPONDENCE

FOR ADDRESS ONLY

NORTHERN PUBLISHING SERVICES

The Llandudno and Colwyn Bay Electric Railway – 1907-1956

SUNNY HILL, LLANDUDNO (c.1908)
Car No.3 just entering Bodafon Fields.
The large building was a Dr. Barnardo's
home for awhile.

POST CARD

FOR CORRESPONDENCE

FOR ADDRESS ONLY

NORTHERN PUBLISHING SERVICES

The Llandudno and Colwyn Bay Electric Railway – 1907-1956

THE TRAMWAY AT SUNNY HILL (c.1910)

An excellent view of the two cars passing each other in the 'loop' in Bodafon Fields from Llandudno. Notice another car waiting in the 'loop' further along the line.

3

POST CARD

FOR CORRESPONDENCE

FOR ADDRESS ONLY

NORTHERN PUBLISHING SERVICES

The Llandudno and Colwyn Bay Electric Railway – 1907-1956

LITTLE ORME, LLANDUDNO (c.1908)
Car No.3 entering Bodafon Fields from Llandudno. Notice another car waiting in the 'loop' further along the line.

MUSIC DEPOT

POST CARD

FOR CORRESPONDENCE

FOR ADDRESS ONLY

NORTHERN PUBLISHING SERVICES

The Llandudno and Colwyn Bay Electric Railway – 1907-1956

MOSTYN STREET, LLANDUDNO (c.1908)
Car No.10 passing the Vaughan Street end of Mostyn Street, Llandudno.

Mostyn Street, Llandudno

POST CARD

FOR CORRESPONDENCE

FOR ADDRESS ONLY

NORTHERN PUBLISHING SERVICES

The Llandudno and Colwyn Bay Electric Railway – 1907-1956

MOSTYN STREET, LLANDUDNO (c.1909)
Car No.9 passes the Domestic Bazar Co.; 'The finest selection in the world at 6½d' it boasts. Now we have Marks & Spencers.

SWISS
CAFÉ

POST CARD

FOR CORRESPONDENCE

FOR ADDRESS ONLY

NORTHERN PUBLISHING SERVICES
The Llandudno and Colwyn Bay Electric Railway – 1907-1956

LLANDUDNO (1907)
Llandudno's first Public Tram Car in Mostyn Street, on 19th October, 1907.

ESTAB
SPIRITS
GROCERY
T. ESMOR

POST CARD

FOR CORRESPONDENCE

FOR ADDRESS ONLY

NORTHERN PUBLISHING SERVICES

The Llandudno and Colwyn Bay Electric Railway – 1907-1956

GLODDAETH AVENUE (c.1910)

Car No.11 leaving Gloddaeth Avenue, Llandudno on its way to Colwyn Bay. Notice how little traffic is about.

I STEAD & SIMPSO
48516. J.V.

POST CARD

FOR CORRESPONDENCE

FOR ADDRESS ONLY

NORTHERN PUBLISHING SERVICES

The Llandudno and Colwyn Bay Electric Railway – 1907-1956

MOSTYN STREET, LLANDUDNO (c.1912)

An excellent view of cars passing in Mostyn Steet. Two policemen wait – but where is the traffic?

POST CARD

FOR CORRESPONDENCE

FOR ADDRESS ONLY

NORTHERN PUBLISHING SERVICES
The Llandudno and Colwyn Bay Electric Railway – 1907-1956

GLODDAETH AVENUE, LLANDUDNO (c.1910)
A car on its way towards West Shore. Notice single track and also the steamer in the Bay.

POST CARD

FOR CORRESPONDENCE | FOR ADDRESS ONLY

NORTHERN PUBLISHING SERVICES

The Llandudno and Colwyn Bay Electric Railway – 1907-1956

INTERIOR OF CAR No.8

The late Reg Johnson and his conductor John Glyn Jones resting between journeys at the West Shore terminus.